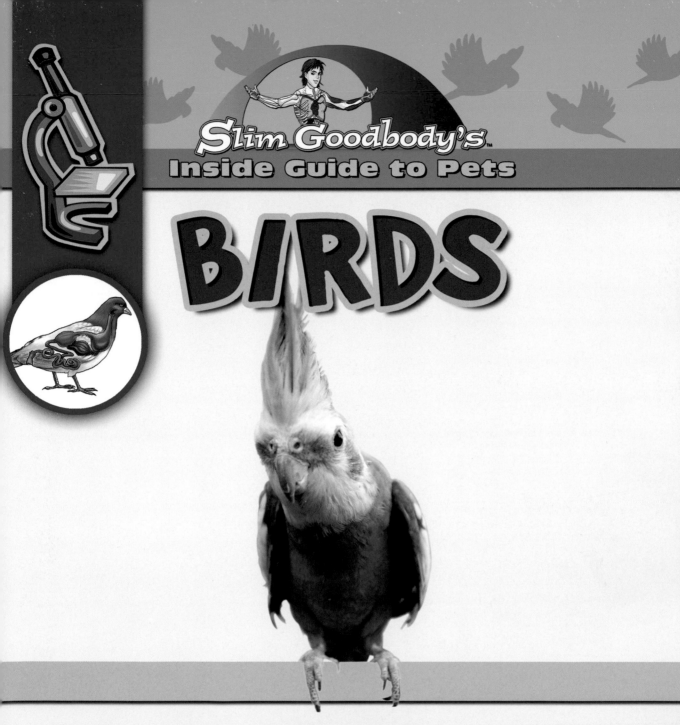

Slim Goodbody's
Inside Guide to Pets

BIRDS

By Slim Goodbody

Illustrations: Ben McGinnis

Consultant: Kate Bergen Pierce,
Doctor of Veterinary Medicine

Gareth Stevens
Publishing

Dedication: For Pecky and Alexander, with love.

Please visit our web site at: www.garethstevens.com
For a free color catalog describing Gareth Stevens Publishing's list
of high-quality books, call 1-800-542-2595 (USA) or 1-800-387-3178 (Canada).
Gareth Stevens Publishing's fax: 1-877-542-2596

Library of Congress Cataloging-in-Publication Data

Burstein, John.
    Birds / John Burstein.
      p. cm. — (Slim Goodbody's inside guide to pets)
    Includes bibliographical references and index.
    ISBN-10: 0-8368-8953-3   ISBN-13: 978-0-8368-8953-6 (lib. bdg.)
  1. Cage birds—Juvenile literature. I. Title.
  SF461.35.B87 2008
  636.6'8—dc22   2007033454

This edition first published in 2008 by
Gareth Stevens Publishing
A Weekly Reader® Company
1 Reader's Digest Road
Pleasantville, NY 10570-7000 USA

Copyright © 2008 by Gareth Stevens, Inc.
Text and artwork copyright © 2008 by Slim Goodbody Corp. (www.slimgoodbody.com).
Slim Goodbody is a registered trademark of Slim Goodbody Corp.

Photos: All photos from iStock Photos except p. 6 (top) courtesy of Digital Morphology
Illustrations: Ben McGinnis, Adventure Advertising

Managing Editor: Valerie J. Weber, Wordsmith Ink
Designer: Tammy West, Westgraphix LLC
Gareth Stevens Senior Managing Editor: Lisa M. Guidone
Gareth Stevens Creative Director: Lisa Donovan

Printed in the United States of America

1 2 3 4 5 6 7 8 9 10 10 09 08

Words that appear in the glossary are printed in **boldface** type the first time they occur in the text.

GREETINGS, BIRD BUDDIES!

Hello there, human friend. My name is Homer. I'm one of the more than 15 million pet birds that live in homes all across the United States and Canada.

Birds are so popular because we make such great pets. We are friendly, loving, beautiful, easy to take care of, and fun to watch. Another bonus — some of us sing beautifully.

Of course, there are many kinds of pet birds. I've made a list of the ten most popular, starting with me. I'm a cockatiel.

1 Cockatiel

2 Parakeet

3 Finch

4 Parrot

5 Lovebird

6 Conure

7 Amazon parrot

8 Canary

9 Dove

10 Cockatoo

Since **ancient** times, people have respected and honored birds. The early Egyptians worshipped a falcon god named Horus. Early Native Americans carved bird pictures on rocks.

First Air Mail

During the 1100s, the Asian **conqueror** Genghis Khan used homing pigeons to carry messages across Asia and Europe. Homing pigeons can find their way home over long distances. As they traveled, Genghis Khan's soldiers would carry homing pigeons with them. If they needed to send a message quickly, they would tie a note to the bird's foot. They then sent the bird winging back to head-quarters. I guess you could say this was the first air mail!

I think that the main reason people like birds so much is that we can do something you can only dream about. We can spread our wings and *fly!*

FUN FACT
There are more than 9,500 different kinds of birds. Like human beings, birds live almost everywhere on Earth — from the frozen polar zones to deserts to steaming rain forests.

Homer's Hints
Some birds are talkers, some birds are squawkers, some sing, and some stay pretty quiet. Some birds need a big cage, some need a small cage. Some birds need lots of attention and some just a little. Before choosing a pet bird, do your homework and learn which kind will be the best match for you and your family.

A skeleton gives an animal's body its basic shape.

A skeleton also holds you up and protects your soft inner parts.

How a skeleton is built affects how an animal is able to move. For example, I need to be light to fly. A heavy bird has a hard time getting off the ground and flying through the air. Most of my bones are thin, helping my body stay light. Some of my bones are actually hollow and contain air sacs.

The biggest and strongest bones in my body are my breast and shoulder bones. These bones support the beating of my wings. My breastbone is called my keel. I also have two bones in each **forearm** that help hold up my wings.

FOREARM BONES

KEEL

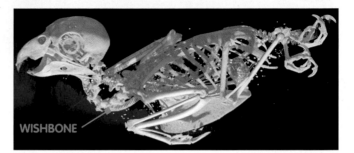

WISHBONE

Wishbones and Wings

I have fewer **joints** than you do because many of my bones are **fused** together. For example, you have two separate collarbones. My two collarbones are joined. You call this part of a bird its *wishbone*. Fewer joints means I need fewer muscles to hold my bones together. Fewer muscles means I have less weight to carry in flight.

When bones are fused, they make a skeleton stiffer. A stiffer skeleton can be helpful. To see what I mean, imagine your arms are wings. Stick them straight out to your sides and flap them up and down. What would happen if you were flying in a strong wind and your wrists bent up or down? You would probably crash! My wrist and hand bones are fused and can't bend like yours do. I can count on them to keep me flying.

My leg bones are also strong. They support my body when I take off, land, run, and hop.

Homer's Hints

Since bird bones are thin, it is important to hold your pet bird carefully. Squeezing too hard might break one of her bones.

I need strong muscles to fly. My strongest muscles attach my chest to my upper arms. These muscles flap my wings. The strength of my flapping wings lifts my body up into the air and keeps it there.

Push Up, Up, and Away!

To get an idea of how strong my chest muscles are, think about doing push-ups. When you do a push-up, your hands are on the floor directly beneath your shoulders. Your chest muscles push straight up. Now, imagine your arms were way, way out from your sides. With your arms stretched, would your chest muscles be strong enough to lift your body and hold it up? Probably not. My chest muscles, however, are powerful enough to lift my body off the ground and into the air!

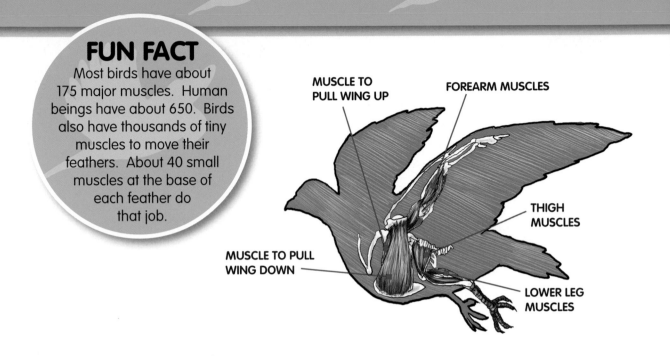

FUN FACT
Most birds have about 175 major muscles. Human beings have about 650. Birds also have thousands of tiny muscles to move their feathers. About 40 small muscles at the base of each feather do that job.

MUSCLE TO PULL WING UP

FOREARM MUSCLES

THIGH MUSCLES

MUSCLE TO PULL WING DOWN

LOWER LEG MUSCLES

One of the reasons my chest muscles can do more than yours is that mine are a bigger part of my body. If a human weighs 100 pounds (45 kilograms), his or her chest muscles weigh about 1 pound (.45 kg). If a bird weighed 100 pounds (45 kg), its chest muscles would weigh 15 pounds (6.8 kg)!

Of course, not all of my muscles are used for flight. I also have strong leg muscles to help me walk, hop, or swim.

Homer's Hints

Your bird needs exercise. Be sure his cage is big enough, so he can climb around inside. Also, give him toys to play with, such as balls, rattles, and bells. Ropes and swings allow him to hang and climb, which is terrific exercise.

When possible, let him out of his cage to play with him. If you let your bird fly around the house for exercise, make sure he's safe. Close the curtains because he won't see the glass and will try to fly outdoors. Make sure that all ceiling fans are off and that there are no hot items on the stove. Close the lid on your toilets, too, so he does not fall in and drown.

My heart looks a lot like yours and does the same job. It pumps blood through my body.

My heart is much bigger than yours, though. I do not mean bigger in actual size; I mean it's bigger compared to the rest of my body. If you were my size, your heart would be only half as big as mine.

My heart also beats a lot faster than yours. The fastest a human heart can beat is about 220 times per minute. When a bird is flying, its heart can beat over 1,000 times per minute. The reason my heart must beat so fast is that flying muscles need lots of energy. A fast-beating heart pumps blood faster. The faster my blood flows, the faster food and oxygen can be turned into energy in my **digestive system**. The faster energy is made, the sooner it reaches my flying muscles.

220

1,000

Lungs and Air Sacs

I breathe a lot faster than you do. If you just ran a race, you might pant at a rate of 80 to 90 times per minute. When I'm flying, I might breathe 450 times per minute!

   I also breathe a little differently than you do. While we both have two lungs, I also have air sacs. When I take a breath of fresh air, half of it goes into my lungs and the other half goes into my air sacs. As I breathe out, the fresh air from the air sacs moves into my lungs. With this system, I always have fresh air in my lungs — when I breathe in AND when I breathe out. This fresh air has lots of oxygen, which I need to make energy.

FUN FACT
Birds do not sweat. We rely on the fresh air that is always moving through our air sacs to keep us cool.

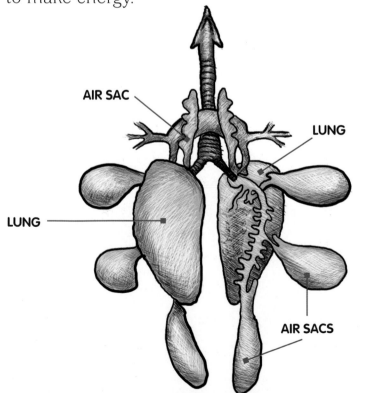

AIR SAC

LUNG

LUNG

AIR SACS

Homer's Hints

Keep your bird away from cooking areas. Some oils, nonstick cooking sprays, and nonstick pans can give off deadly fumes if they are overheated. If your bird breathes in these fumes, she can die.

A GRINDING GIZZARD

STOMACH

GIZZARD

CROP

HUMAN DIGESTIVE SYSTEM

STOMACH

Humans and birds both have a digestive system that breaks food down into tiny pieces to be used for energy. My digestive system looks a lot like yours, but there are some important differences. For example, I have two stomachs! You have only one. My lower stomach is called my gizzard. This tough, **muscular** organ crushes and grinds up food. I have no teeth, so my gizzard's work is important. Sometimes I swallow grit or gravel to help my gizzard do its job. When I eat something hard and tough like a seed, my gizzard muscles grind it against the grit and gravel. The grinding action smashes the seed, breaking it into tiny bits that I can digest.

Many birds have an extra organ called a crop. It acts like a storage bin. Food reaches the crop before it gets to the stomach. Birds can eat in a hurry, store food in the crop, and later find a safe place to digest the stored food.

This ability is very important. If we spend too long staying in one place and eating, an enemy has a better chance of pouncing on us.

Homer's Hints

Your bird needs vitamin A to stay healthy. It keeps his feathers, skin, eyes, digestive system, and lungs in top condition. Seeds don't have enough vitamin A, so you need to add vitamin A-rich foods to his diet every day. Sweet potatoes, squash, carrots, spinach, corn, apricots, and eggs are all good sources of vitamin A.

NEAT FEET

Look at your foot. You have five toes. They all point in the same direction — straight ahead. I have only four toes, and one of them points backward! My other three toes are usually spread wide apart. Widely spread toes let me wrap my feet around a branch and grasp it tightly.

I also use my feet to grab food and lift it to my mouth. When I hold food, I pull my toes closer together.

Homer's Hints

Your bird's claws will need to be trimmed when they get too long. Trimming with a clipper or scissors is not hard, but you can easily hurt your bird's feet. Only adults should trim a bird's claws.

My feet are curved and covered with a tough kind of skin called scales. They end in strong, sharp claws.

I use my feet to hop and walk. My feet tell me what kind of surface I am on, for example, rough or smooth.

A Great Grip

My feet also have a special design perfect for perching. When I sit, they lock tightly around my perch. If I fall asleep, I won't fall off! When I wake up and stand, my feet let go.

My legs and feet are gray. Legs and feet can also come in different colors, including white, black, brown, tan, pink, and even yellow!

Birds are the only animals in the whole world that have feathers. I think that's pretty cool.

My feathers are perfectly designed for flying. They are **lightweight** but very strong. They are **flexible** but tough.

I have two main kinds of feathers:

My down feathers are the small, fluffy feathers right next to my skin. They trap my body heat to help keep me warm and dry.

My contour feathers cover and protect my body. Contour feathers give me my nice round shape and my color. Contour feathers help me fly. Their center **shaft** is hollow. Rows of branches called barbs line the shaft.

Branching off each barb are hundreds of tinier barbs called barbules. Barbules from one feather can hook onto barbules from another feather, holding both feathers together. All the barbs and barbules together is called the vane of the wing. At the base of each feather are tiny muscles that move it.

BARBS

SHAFT   **BARBULES**

16

Friends and Feathers

When my feathers are fully grown, blood stops flowing through them. They die. They're like your hair or fingernails. Feathers are even made of the same material as your hair and nails. It's called keratin.

I spend a lot of time caring for my feathers, or preening. I also preen my friends' feathers sometimes. I use my feet and beak to keep them all lined up nice and tight.

Homer's Hints

Your bird likes to keep her feathers clean. Be sure to give her enough water to take a regular bath. Just fill a small bowl with water, and she'll have a great time. After a bath, let her dry off completely in a warm area.

A PEAK AT BEAKS

Different types of birds have different types of beaks and eat different kinds of food. What they eat depends on the length, shape, and thickness of their beaks.

I have a short, hard, cone-shaped beak. It's very strong. I use it to break open tough seeds. I depend upon my beak to tear or crush food into small enough chunks to swallow. Remember, I have no teeth.

Birds' beaks grow during their entire lives. The tip wears out from all the use and must keep being replaced.

Tongue and Taste

Inside their beaks, most birds have tongues. A bird's tongue usually has five bones in it. These bones give it strength but not much flexibility. Your tongue is different. It is made of muscle and is very flexible.

The taste of food is not very important to me. As a matter of fact, I have less than three hundred **taste buds** on my tongue. They send messages to my brain about flavor. You have about nine thousand taste buds on your tongue. Your taste buds are located in many places on your tongue. My taste buds are located at the back of my tongue.

Homer's Hints

Wild birds wear down their beaks on bark, rocks, or other hard surfaces. Birds in cages don't have these hard surfaces. Their beaks can grow too long. Putting a **cuttlebone** in their cages can help. When your bird pecks at this hard shell, his beak gets a natural trimming.

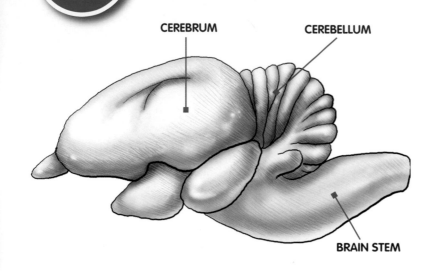

CEREBRUM   CEREBELLUM

BRAIN STEM

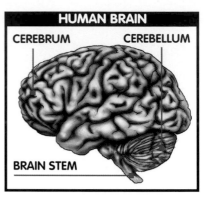

HUMAN BRAIN

CEREBRUM   CEREBELLUM

BRAIN STEM

My brain and your brain have a lot in common. For example

 They are both protected inside a bony skull.

 They both have a cerebrum, a cerebellum, and a brain stem.

 They are both connected to nerves that branch out through the body.

The major difference between our brains is in the cerebrum. The cerebrum is the part of the brain responsible for thinking. Your cerebrum is a big part of your brain. Thinking is not as important to me as it is to you, so my cerebrum is a much smaller part of my brain. I can, however, find food, avoid danger, build a nest, and find my way home.

FUN FACT

A bird's brain weighs about ten times as much as a brain of a reptile of the same weight. If I weighed the same as a frog, my brain would weigh ten times as much as its brain.

More Folds, Smarter Brain

My cerebrum is smooth. Your cerebrum has lots of folds. Folds allow more information to be packed into the same space.

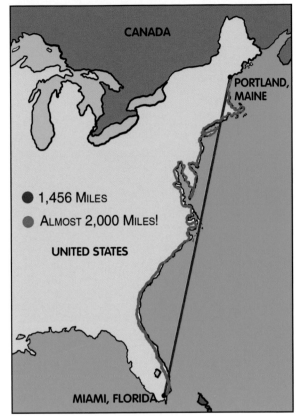

- 1,456 Miles
- Almost 2,000 Miles!

UNITED STATES

CANADA

PORTLAND, MAINE

MIAMI, FLORIDA

Think of the coastline of the United States. If you travel in a straight line, the distance between the cities of Portland, Maine, and Miami, Florida, is 1,456 miles (2,343 kilometers). However, if you travel along the coast, which winds and folds, the distance is almost 2,000 miles (3,219 km). If each mile stood for a piece of information, think how much more you would learn traveling along the coast instead of going in a straight line!

My cerebellum is equal in ability to yours, however. The cerebellum is the part of the brain that controls muscle movement. My cerebellum is well developed because it controls flying. A complex process, flying takes balance and lots of muscle **coordination**.

Our brain stems are pretty equal in power as well. The brain stem controls the beating of our hearts, breathing, digestion, and other processes inside our bodies.

Homer's Hints

Lots of birds are smart enough to learn tricks. Some can even learn to talk. All it takes is practice. Remember, it took you a long time to learn how to walk and talk. If you take the time, your bird will learn.

My eyes are HUGE compared to the size of my head. If my head were as big as yours, my eyes would be fifteen times larger than your eyes are. Large eyes allow me to see more at one time.

Both of your eyes face forward. This position lets both of your eyes focus together on one object. My eyes are placed out on the sides of my head. Each eye sees a different picture. This position gives me a wider range of vision than yours. This wide range allows me to see danger coming from two sides at the same time. Unfortunately, my vision makes it harder to see what is right in front of me.

AREA SEEN BY RIGHT EYE

AREA SEEN BY LEFT EYE

AREA SEEN BY BOTH EYES

And the Winner Is . . .

My eye muscles are quicker and stronger than yours. If we both stood on a hill and had a contest to see who could spot more things in a minute, I would win claws down. I can also see more shades of color than you can.

I depend upon my sight more than any of my other senses. It helps me fly and land. It also helps me find food and avoid danger.

Homer's Hints

Let your bird look out the window. She will enjoy looking at nature. Besides, birds need sunlight. Sunlight helps her skin stay healthy and her bones strong. Place her cage in a sunny spot that gets lots of air. On hot summer days, cover a small area of the cage to give her some shade if she feels too hot.

23

LISTEN HEAR

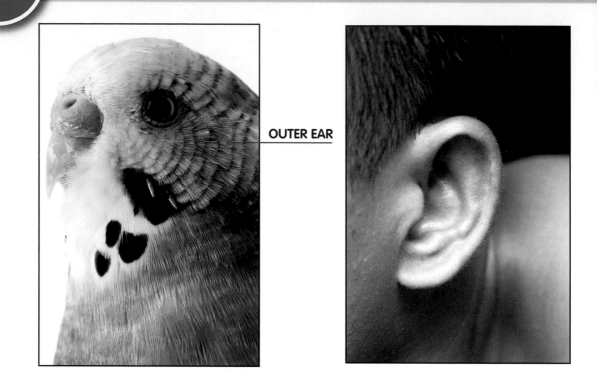

OUTER EAR

My ear and your ear both have three parts — an outer ear, a middle ear, and an inner ear. When you look at me, you cannot see my outer ear! It's just a short tube leading to my **eardrum**. Special feathers that let sound through cover my outer ear.

I have one bone in my middle ear. You have three.

My inner ear has three **semicircular** canals. There is fluid in the canals. When I move my head, the fluid moves. This movement sends a message to my brain that helps me keep my balance. Your inner ear works in the same way.

SEMICIRCULAR CANALS

FUN FACT

A barn owl can locate and catch a tiny mouse by sound alone. It can do this in complete darkness — from half a block away!

Swift Sounds

In some ways, I can hear better than you can. For example, you can hear sounds that last about one-twentieth of a second. I can hear sounds that last only one two-hundredth of a second. Sometimes I can hear ten separate notes in the time it takes you to hear only one note.

In other ways, our sense of hearing is pretty equal. For example, if a sound is too far away for you to hear, I will not be able to hear it either.

Almost all birds make sounds, which they use to communicate. Sounds help birds recognize each other. They also let birds know if there is danger or food nearby.

Homer's Hints

Leave the radio on when you leave your bird alone. He will enjoy listening to some soft music or talk. Just be sure not to keep your radio too loud.

IN TOUCH

Humans and birds both rely upon their sense of touch to get important information. Touch tells us about our world. For example, it lets us know what is soft, hard, smooth, or sharp.

My skin has special nerve endings. These nerve endings send messages about touch to my brain. Some parts of my body have more nerve endings than others. I have lots of nerve endings on the inside of my mouth and on my tongue, beak, and feet. A sense of touch in these places helps me the most. For example, nerves in my feet help me know what kind of surface I am holding on to. That way, I know how hard to grip. Nerves in my beak help me know how hard a seed is, so I can crack it open easily.

I can also feel **vibrations** in my legs. This feeling tells me when a bird is coming near me on the ground or on a tree limb. Some human scientists think that this ability to sense faint vibrations may be the reason I seem to know when an earthquake is about to happen. I can feel it long before you humans have any sense of it.

Smell

I cannot brag about my sense of smell. I do not even have a nose! My nostrils are located near the base of my beak. The only job my nostrils have is breathing — not smelling.

27

AMAZING FACTS

I hope you have enjoyed learning more about birds. Of course, I could not cover everything in one book. It would take a whole encyclopedia. Thousands of scientists all over the world study birds. I thought it would be fun to leave you with some amazing facts these scientists have discovered.

 Some hummingbirds flap their wings as many as one hundred times per second.

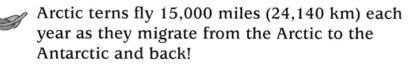 The world's smallest bird is the bee humming-bird. It is 2 ½ inches (6.3 centimeters) long and weighs only 0.08 ounces (less than 3 grams). That's a little less than the weight of a dime!

 The wandering albatross has an 11-foot (3.3-meter) wingspan.

 Arctic terns fly 15,000 miles (24,140 km) each year as they migrate from the Arctic to the Antarctic and back!

 One parakeet learned seventeen hundred words by the time he was four years old.

In 1861, a **fossil** of Archaeopteryx, the first known bird, was discovered. It lived 140 million years ago.

About one-third of a bird's feathers are on its head.

With a total of only 940 feathers, the ruby-hummingbird is the bird with the least feathers.

 The bird with the most feathers is the whistling, or tundra, swan. During winter, it can have as many as twenty-five thousand feathers.

The longest feather ever measured was a tail feather that was 34 ¾ feet long (10.6 m). It belonged to a special kind of chicken raised in Japan.

 The largest beak in the world belongs to the Australian pelican, which can be as long as 18 ½ inches (47 cm).

 The sword-billed hummingbird has a beak longer than the rest of its body.

The black woodpecker strikes its bill against a tree between eight and twelve thousand times a day.

Guinea fowl and waterfowl have such great hearing that they have been used as watchdogs throughout history.

 Long-lived birds such as macaws can sometimes survive as long as one hundred years.

 An eagle can spot food while flying 1 mile (1.6 km) above the earth.

Some birds have eyes that are so large, they weigh more than their brain.

Some birds have amazing memories. One kind of North American crow collects up to thirty thousand pine seeds over three weeks in November. It then carefully buries them for safekeeping across an area of 200 square miles (520 square kilometers). Over the next eight months, it is able to find 90 percent of them, even when they are covered under several feet of snow.

GLOSSARY

ancient — relating to a time long ago

conqueror — someone who defeats a country or a people

coordination — the act of working together smoothly

cuttlebone — the inner shell of a cuttlefish

digestive system — the group of organs, including the stomach and the intestines, that breaks down food and changes it into energy that the body needs

eardrum — a special thin layer of skin that separates the outer and middle ear and carries sound waves to the tiny bones in the middle ear

flexible — able to bend easily

forearm — the part of the arm between the elbow and the wrist or a similar part in other animals with backbones

fossil — the remains or imprint of prehistoric plants or animals found in rock, coal, tar, volcanic ash, or frozen in ice

fused — joined together

joints — places in the body where two or more bones meet

lightweight — weighing very little

muscular — made up of strong muscles

semicircular — having a half-circle shape

shaft — the long, thin stem that runs lengthwise through a feather

taste buds — nerve endings that send information about flavors to the brain

vibrations — rapid motions back and forth or from side to side

FOR MORE INFORMATION

BOOKS

Bird World. Pet's Point of View (series). Meredith Phillips (Compass Point Books)

Brilliant Birds. Perfect Pets (series). Mary Elizabeth Salzmann (Abdo Publishing Company)

Caring for Your Bird. Caring for Your Pet (series). Lynn Hamilton (Weigl Educational Publishers)

My First Bird. My First Pet Library from the American Humane Association (series). Linda Bozzo (Enslow Elementary)

WEB SITES

ASPCA Animaland Pet Care
www.aspca.org/site/PageServer?pagename = kids_pc_bird_411
Learn how to care for various pet birds at this Web site for kids who love animals! You can also click on a link to watch Pet Care Cartoons.

Backyard Birds
www.backyardnature.net/birds.htm
Learn about the birds in your own backyard and how their bodies work.

Budgies
www.bbc.co.uk/cbbc/wild/pets/budgie.shtml
Click on this cool site with games and information to learn loads about your budgie, or parakeet, and its behavior.

INDEX

DEC - - 2008

ABOUT THE AUTHOR

John Burstein (also known as Slim Goodbody) has been entertaining and educating children for over thirty years. His programs have been broadcast on CBS, PBS, Nickelodeon, USA, and Discovery. He has won numerous awards including the Parent's Choice Award and the President's Council's Fitness Leader Award. Currently, Mr. Burstein tours the country with his multimedia live show "Bodyology." For more information, please visit slimgoodbody.com.